GRANDFATHER FOUR WINDS AND RIS
CHANIN MICHAEL   ECHA   16167

D1316992

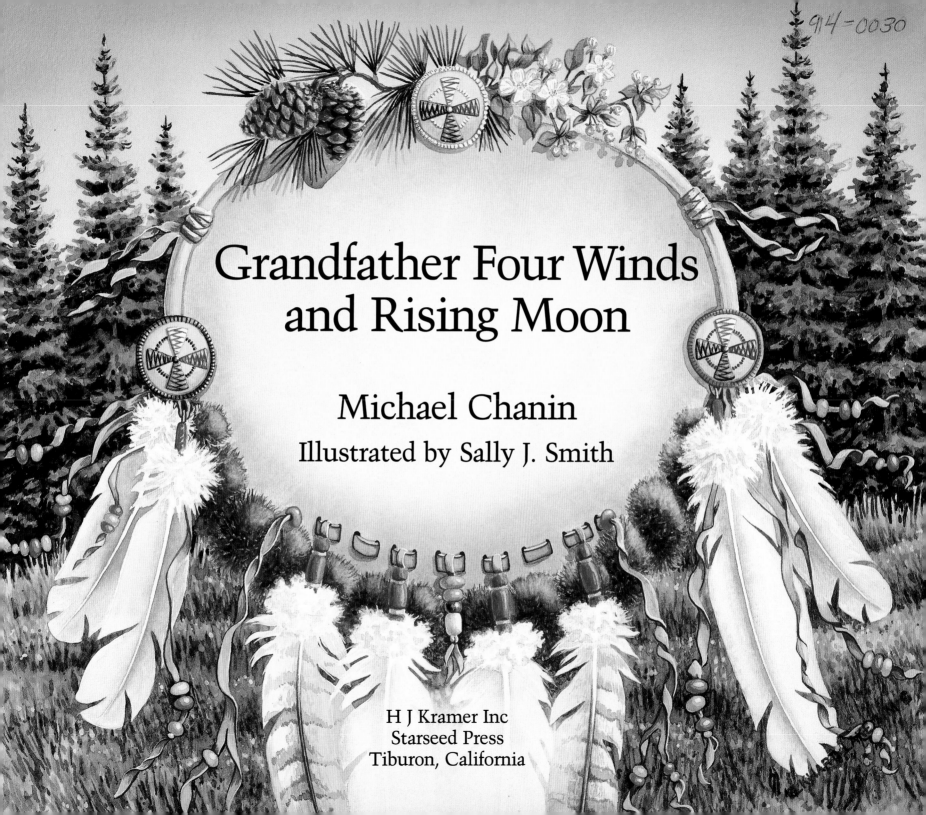

914-0030

Grandfather Four Winds and Rising Moon

Michael Chanin

Illustrated by Sally J. Smith

H J Kramer Inc
Starseed Press
Tiburon, California

To Sri Yukteswar and Grandmother,
for without their teachings
this book would not have been written.
M. C.

With love to
Dolly, Mickey, Lillybuff, Robbie, Ace, Cal,
and especially Robert.
To the Great Spirit in us all. Namasté.
S. J. S.

There once was a grandfather named Four Winds. He was blind. He had a grandson whose name was Rising Moon. Often they would sit on a cliff high above the valley floor, and the boy would tell his grandfather what he saw.

Sometimes Rising Moon would shout, "Grandfather, I see deer grazing on the grass." Or he would say, "I see black clouds with their bellies full of water." Other times the boy would jump up and down and yell, "Grandfather, I see the great eagle soaring on the wind that blows from the east."

One day, while walking in the valley, Rising Moon did not see any deer, eagles, or clouds. He felt no wind. It had not rained for a long time, and the land was dry. Rising Moon told his grandfather what he saw. "Grandfather Four Winds, the land is parched and thirsty. The earth is cracked. The river is muddy, and the grass is brown. The eagle flies no more, and the deer are gone."

Grandfather Four Winds, his sightless face turned toward the blazing sun, said to the boy, "Grandson, what you see frightens you. What are you afraid of?"

"I am afraid that our people will go without food and water. I am afraid that the deer and all the four-legged ones will die. I am afraid that my home will be no more."

The old man touched the boy's face and said in a gentle voice, "Rising Moon, because you are old enough to fret and worry, you are old enough to pray. It is time to visit our sacred spot."

Four Winds and Rising Moon had a special place where they sometimes sat underneath a great tree. The tree was very old and charred from fire. Her branches stretched to the ground and surrounded them like a teepee. Since the fire, Grandfather Four Winds called this tree the Tree of Our People. While they sat under her branches, he told Rising Moon a story from long ago.

"Once, Rising Moon, when I was a young boy, a great pine tree full of needles and cones stood next to a much smaller and younger apple tree.

"The story begins in winter
during the time of the great snows when the
nights are long and dark. One very cold night, Pine Tree
said to Apple Tree, 'You silly tree, you have lost all of your
leaves. It's very cold now. The wind is blowing, and the snow is falling.
Without your leaves, what is going to keep your branches from feeling
frozen and stiff? You should be like me. I never let go of my needles. They keep
me warm in the season of ice.'

"Apple Tree replied, 'It is my
nature to stand bare in the winter.
Standing with my naked branches,
I learn the gift of courage and strength.
When the cold winds howl and my branches
bend, I howl back with the sound of a hundred bears.'

"Pine Tree thought Apple Tree was a fool, but
that did not sway Apple Tree. She stood tall next to
Pine Tree because winter was her time of courage."

Grandfather Four Winds stopped telling the story for a moment. He felt the wind as it began to blow ever so slightly. It was like a whisper that the boy beside him could not hear.

"The story continues in spring, my frightened grandson," said the old man. "This was the time of year when Apple Tree bloomed with leaf and flower. Her leaves were green and tender. Her sweetly scented flowers were white with pink edges.

"Pine Tree, who
was feeling jealous, sneered at
Apple Tree and asked, 'What are those
funny little white things hanging from
your skinny branches, Apple Tree?'

"'They are my flowers, Pine Tree.
Bees delight in them, and their
fragrance fills the air with a sweet scent,'
answered the young tree patiently.

"'Humph,' snorted the old evergreen.
'What good are they?'

"'What good are they?' Apple Tree chuckled. 'Why, this is springtime, and my wonderful flowers attract many birds and insects. My branches are alive with birdsong and buzzing bees praising this season of spring. I am grateful for the warm sun and the water of spring rain. I am grateful for Great Spirit's gift of flowers and leaves,' said Apple Tree.

"With that, Pine Tree stilled the movement of his branches and stopped talking. Apple Tree hummed softly to herself a sweet song, as sweet as the scent of apple blossoms, for being grateful was the lesson of spring."

Grandfather Four Winds heard the rhythm of Rising Moon's breathing. It was slow and steady, like a drumbeat, and Four Winds knew that the boy was calm and no longer worried about the drought. The old man continued his story.

"In the season of summer, Apple Tree's delicate flowers fell from her branches, painting the ground white. Soon afterward, her apples appeared as little green buds. In time, as the days got longer, the buds grew into small green apples. As the moon passed through the season of the sun, the green apples turned into hearty red ones.

"That summer, Apple Tree was proud of her fruit. She felt as if she were a mother and the apples were her children! She tended them with care. She fed them through her roots, which drank heartily from the rich earth.

"One morning, Apple Tree awoke and was excited because it was time for her fruit to be picked. First, the children of the tribe picked the apples. Then, one by one, Apple Tree gave her fruit freely to all of the people. Each time an apple was picked, Apple Tree laughed a full laugh, for she felt as if she were being tickled.

"'Humph,' snorted Pine Tree. 'How can you laugh when these people are stealing the fruit from your branches?'

"'They are not stealing my fruit,' replied Apple Tree. 'Summer is my give-away time. I am happy to give my fruit to the people. My apples are my gift to life, and the people give me the gift of joy when they eat them. That is why I laugh so much in the summer,' said Apple Tree.

"Pine Tree snorted again. He held onto his pinecones and shook his branches so hard that all of the squirrels came tumbling to the ground."

Grandfather Four Winds paused and felt
the change of the weather on his skin. He
could feel that clouds were starting to
move into the valley. Rising Moon
moved closer to the old man to keep
himself warm. Then Four Winds continued
his story with the final season, autumn.

"In the fall, the lesson for Apple Tree is faith. It is the season when Apple Tree drops all of her leaves. She gives them back to our mother, the Earth.

"'Apple Tree, Apple Tree, aren't you afraid that your leaves will never grow back?' asked Pine Tree.

"'No, no, my friend,' replied Apple Tree. 'I have faith that my leaves will grow again in the light of the spring sun. Faith allows me to let go of my precious coat of green.'

"'Humph,' snorted Pine Tree as he held on tightly to his pine needles. 'I don't believe in having faith. I think you are a fool, little tree.'

"But Apple Tree did not let Pine Tree spoil her jovial mood. She was happy to know faith, and she danced in the autumn breeze as the wind scattered her leaves over the valley floor."

ELKHART LAKE I M C

Grandfather Four Winds
heard a clap of thunder in
the distance. Blue Jay
squawked. She heard it,
too. But Rising Moon was
so involved with the story
that he did not stir.

"I don't like Pine Tree.
He is mean," said the boy.

The old man raised his arms above his head and waved them back and forth. They looked like trees swaying in the breeze. "Rising Moon," said Four Winds, "Pine Tree's wisdom is towering strength. He shows us how to stand tall in the deepest valleys and on the highest mountains. He teaches us how to withstand the fiercest winds. Grandson, in his own way, Pine Tree helped Apple Tree become the best tree she could be."

"Grandfather Four Winds," said Rising Moon, "you are blind. How could you see the changes in Apple Tree?"

The old man answered, "My ears are like those of a deer. I hear many sounds that you don't hear. I listen when my brothers and sisters talk to me. I have heard Apple Tree's laughter, her howl, and her song. I have felt her joy in the dancing leaves. I have learned a great deal from my sister, Apple Tree."

"Whatever happened to her?" asked Rising Moon. Grandfather Four Winds held his grandson close now, for he, too, was feeling the coolness of the breeze. "Rising Moon, there was once a great fire in the valley. It happened before you were born. Much of the forest was ablaze with fire. Pine Tree died.

"But little Apple Tree survived.
The flames charred her bark, and she never bore fruit again. But she spoke to me after the fire. She was now like a medicine woman, wise and regal," said Grandfather Four Winds. "She would say to me, 'Blind man who knows how to listen, come sit underneath my branches. My fruit is no longer my apples. Now my fruit is my words, so listen closely.'

"Rising Moon,
we sit under her right
now. This sacred tree, the Tree
of Our People, is old Apple Tree," said
Grandfather Four Winds. "Even now she whispers
to me—and to you. She says, 'Rising Moon, grandson of Four
Winds, live like the apple tree: Know the courage, the gratitude,
the give-away, and the faith within your own heart. Use these teachings
in your life.'" Rising Moon looked up at Apple Tree and thanked her for her wisdom.

Grandfather Four Winds continued: "Grandson, Apple
Tree has asked you to stand now and face the heavens."
Rising Moon stood, turned his face to the sky, and felt
the first drops of rain.

All children are seeds from the stars
who look to adults for love, inspiration, guidance, and
the promise of a safe and friendly world. We dedicate Starseed
Press to this vision and to the sacred child in each of us.

Hal and Linda Kramer,
Publishers

Text copyright © 1994 by Michael Chanin.
Illustrations copyright © 1994 by Sally J. Smith.
All rights reserved. No part of this book may be reproduced or utilized in any form or by any
means, electronic or mechanical, including photocopying, recording, or by any information
storage and retrieval system, without permission in writing from the publisher.

H J Kramer Inc
P.O. Box 1082
Tiburon, CA 94920

Library of Congress Cataloging-in-Publication Data

Chanin, Michael.
    Grandfather Four Winds and Rising Moon / by Michael Chanin ;
illustrated by Sally Smith.
        p. cm.
    Summary: Grandfather Four Winds helps his young grandson learn
the lessons of courage, gratitude, generosity, and faith from the old
apple tree that is sacred to their people.
    ISBN 0-915811-47-2 : $14.95
    [1. Indians of North America—Fiction.   2. Trees—Fiction.
3. Seasons—Fiction.] I. Smith, Sally, ill. II. Title.
PZ7.C35969Gr 1994   93-2689
[E]—dc20   CIP
                                                                 AC

Editor: Nancy Grimley Carleton
Art Director: Linda Kramer
Book Production: Schuettge and Carleton
Composition: Classic Typography
Printed in Hong Kong
10 9 8 7 6 5 4 3 2 1